P9-AOI-283

Guaranteed for Life

Your Rights Under The United States Constitution

Guaranteed

The
CONSTITUTION
of the
UNITED STATES OF
AMERICA

Preamble

WE, the PEOPLE of the UNITED STATES, in order to form a more perfect Union, establish

for Life

Your Rights Under The United States Constitution

by

Bruce Allyn Findlay

PRENTICE-HALL, INC.
Englewood Cliffs, N. J.
1955

Library of Congress
Catalog Card No.: 55-11222

★ ★ ★

Printed in the United States of America

36620

Contents

"Sweet Freedom's Song"– The Unfinished Symphony....... 2

The Eight Basic Principles of Your Government............ 9

Instruments of Freedom vs. Instruments of Tyranny:
Twenty-Five Guarantees.................... 31

Instruments of a Republic: How to Play Your Part........ 87

Constitution of the United States........................ 107

Index.. 131

Guaranteed for Life

by

Bruce Allyn Findlay

"SWEET FREEDOM'S SONG" ___

Living in the United States is like being a member of a great orchestra. Each of the 165 million citizens is a musician playing one or more of the many instruments that make up a complete orchestra.

The basic theme of the music is the United States Constitution. It is the score from which the musicians play. The arrangers, those who interpret the theme and make harmonious additions, are the two houses of Congress. The conductor of this great orchestra is the President whom the players have chosen to lead them.

The friendly critics, who know every note of the symphony, are the members of the Supreme Court. It is their task to check the leader and the arrangers when they have taken too many liberties in their interpretation.

The melody, "Sweet Freedom's Song," has been sung, hummed, played, and whistled by citizens of this nation since the Constitution was completed in 1787.

A successful concert requires much individual practice and numerous rehearsals. The unfinished symphony that you are playing will need in the future, as it has in the past, the voluntary participation and co-operation of all of the musicians. Unless you, the members of this tremendous orchestra, *choose* to follow the score and the leadership you have selected, your *right to choose* is in danger.

With choice, you are free men and women; without it, you are slaves.

There are some citizens who "play by ear." They have never really studied the Constitution. They have little idea of its contents and of what it does mean and of what it can mean. They are carried along with the others. Occasionally they get out of time or tune, but they usually recover rapidly.

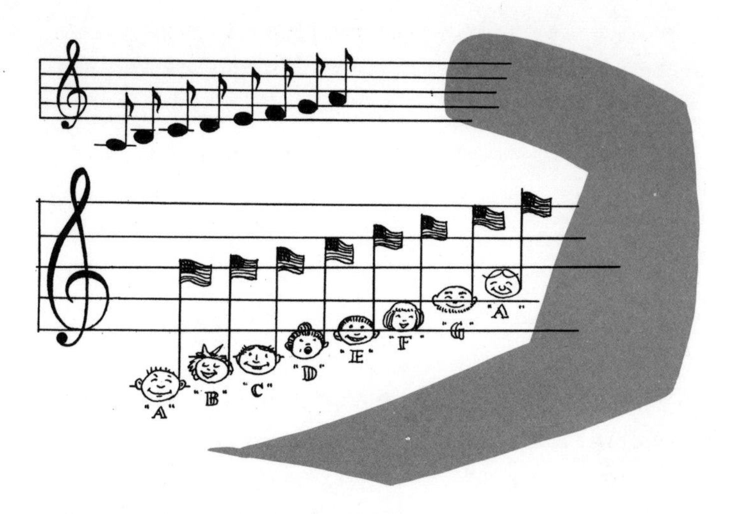

A — *Amending Process*
B — *Balances and Checks*
C — *Constitutional Supremacy*
D — *Dual Form of Government*
E — *Exalted Judiciary*
F — *Freedoms—Civil and Political*
G — *Government of Limited Powers*
A — *A Republican Form of Government*

Contrasted with those who "play by ear" are those who read music thoroughly, who know the Constitution very well, but who intentionally create discord.

Most of the people, however, have great respect for the Constitution, have read or studied it, and sincerely try to be co-operative, helpful citizens. Were it otherwise, you would soon lose your liberties as many other nations have.

Before there can be any melody there must be a scale; otherwise, there would be but a single, monotonous tone.

There are eight notes in the musical scale; there are eight notes in the political scale. Each note represents a basic principle written into your Constitution. Almost unlimited combinations of uses can be, and are, made of these important principles to help you keep your freedom.

The notes in the scale are the basis of all music, but their use alone is not enough to make music satisfying. What would music be without rhythm, tempo, accent, melody, expression, volume, syncopation, tone, rests, phrases, pauses, and many other elements?

To the constitutional scale, as to the musical, much must be added in order to produce the laws that work for the good of the whole orchestra and to make it possible for the laws to be interpreted and enforced.

INSTRUMENTS OF YOUR REPUBLIC

Among the many instruments of your republic that could be named, here are some that are important:

Communications, confidence, co-operation, culture, courage, determination, education, faith, family, generosity, genius, health, hope, initiative, labor, leadership, loyalty, management, resources, responsibility, rewards, savings, skillfulness, spirituality, tolerance, tools. Other instruments could be added.

Important as are the scale and the other factors, there would be no orchestra without instruments, for there would be no way of changing the notes into sweet music.

Some orchestras use many instruments; others use only a few.

All communities are guaranteed the "instruments" necessary to keep "Sweet Freedom's Song" ringing across the nation.

Each citizen belongs to this great orchestra, and each has an important part to play. You have at your command eight great principles — your political scale — and 25 "instruments" — the 25 basic guarantees of your Constitution. What more could you ask?

Why does the average citizen in your nation enjoy more of the good things of life than any other average citizen? Are your "know-how," your inventive genius, your managerial skill, and your ability to solve most of your problems just luck? Are they just the blind turn of the wheel of chance? Are they merely good fortune?

If your Constitution were transplanted without change to many nations now impoverished in the midst of great natural resources, what would happen? Would the peoples of these nations suddenly own radios, television sets, cars, refrigerators, vacuum cleaners, permanent waves, electric razors, and a thousand blessings common to millions of American homes?

When your founding fathers wrote your Constitution, they arranged the "music" so that each generation could add "instruments" and interpretation as needed. The small piccolo is as important as the mighty organ. Protection of life, liberty, and property is guaranteed every citizen, be he humble or great. These three — life, liberty, and property — are the heart of the American Way.

With such granite-like security, is it any wonder this nation has prospered spiritually, culturally, politically, and economically?

The unfinished symphony, ". . . One nation under God, indivisible, with liberty . . .," will continue to echo and re-echo across the nation from coast to coast, from border to border, as it did in 1787 through the thirteen small, courageous states where it originated, if the "musicians" unselfishly, sincerely, intelligently dedicate themselves to play the "music" as it was written by the founding fathers and "rearranged" from time to time by the people and their representatives.

In the two succeeding sections of this book, the left-hand pages will depict and explain what your constitutional guarantees mean to you. The right-hand pages will show what could happen were there no such constitutional guarantees.

George Washington:
"Let us erect a standard to which the wise and honest may repair."

THE EIGHT BASIC PRINCIPLES OF YOUR GOVERNMENT

Fitting the cloth to the need!

AMENDING PROCESS

No greater stroke of genius is to be found in any constitution than the provision for the process of amending your Constitution by peaceful organized methods.

"The Congress . . . shall propose amendments . . . or, on the application . . . of two thirds of the . . . states, shall call a convention for proposing amendments, which . . . shall be valid . . . when ratified by . . . three fourths of the several states. . . ." (Article 5)

NO AMENDING PROCESS

For thousands of years men had to fight and die for every change in government that gave the people more liberty and freedom. Change and revolution were words that meant the same thing.

Then came the great idea of change without revolution — the amending process. In government, because of growth, there are many strains, rips, and tears. All can be repaired by the a-mending process.

There is no excuse for anyone's attempting to overthrow your government in order to make a change.

BALANCES AND CHECKS

Balances

Checks

Checks on Congress:

(a) Change of the House membership possible every two years.

"The House of Representatives shall be . . . chosen every second year. . . ." (Article 1, Section 2)

(b) Money bills must originate in the House.

"All bills for raising revenue shall originate in the House of Representatives. . . ." (Article 1, Section 7)

(c) Any bill originating in the House must be approved by the Senate. (Article 1, Section 7)

(d) Any bill originating in the Senate must be approved by the House. (Article 1, Section 7)

(e) One third of the Senate may be changed every two years. (Article 1, Section 3)

(f) **"Neither House, during the session of Congress, shall, without the consent of the other, adjourn for more than three days. . . ." (Article 1, Section 5)**

(g) **"Each House shall keep a journal of its proceedings. . . ." (Article 1, Section 5)**

(h) The President has the power of veto.

". . . If he [the President] approve he shall sign it, but if not he shall return it, with his objections. . . ." (Article 1, Section 7)

Checks on the President:

(a) The President can be impeached (which means brought to trial).

"The House of Representatives . . . shall have the sole power of impeachment." (Article 1, Section 2)

(b) Laws can be passed over the presidential veto.

". . . if approved by two thirds [of both houses]

it shall become a law. . . ." (Article 1, Section 7)

(c) Military appropriations are limited.

". . . no appropriation . . . [to raise and support armies] shall be for a longer term than two years. . . ." (Article 1, Section 8)

(d) The Senate acts as a Jury to try impeachment cases. (Article 1, Section 3)

(e) Treaty-making power is limited by the Senate. (Article 2, Section 2)

(f) Power of appointment is limited by the Senate. (Article 2, Section 2)

(g) **"The Congress shall assemble at least once in every year. . . ." (Article 1, Section 4)**

Checks on Supreme Court:

(a) Judges are nominated by the President, confirmed by the Senate.

". . . by and with the advice and consent of the Senate, [the President] shall appoint . . . judges of the Supreme Court. . . ." (Article 2, Section 2)

This is an appointive office. The power of the Supreme Court is limited "into jurisdictions" by the Constitution. (Article 3, Section 2)

(b) *Impeachment:* Judges can be impeached.

"The judges . . . shall hold their offices during good behavior. . . ." (Article 3, Section 1)

"The House of Representatives . . . shall have the sole power of impeachment. . . ." The Senate sits as a jury. (Article 1, Section 2)

Checks on Federal Government:

"The enumeration in the Constitution, of certain rights, shall not be construed to deny or disparage others retained by the people."

"The powers not delegated to the United States by the Constitution . . . are reserved to the states respectively, or to the people." (Amendments 9 and 10)

NO BALANCES AND CHECKS

Were there no checks and balances in *your* Constitution, this might happen.

CONSTITUTIONAL SUPREMACY

Your government may be compared to many other things besides an orchestra. As long as the trunk of the Tree of Liberty remains healthy, the limbs have a chance to be healthy. The limbs may need pruning and spraying at times. They bend and may break in the storms, but the Tree will live on and on if the roots are firm and its trunk is solid and vigorous. Extremes of cold and heat, of rain and drought, have strengthened the Tree of Liberty.

If the United States Constitution remains the supreme law of the land, neither subversive termites nor insects can destroy the Tree or its branches.

The Tree of Liberty will not stand too much grafting.

"This Constitution . . . shall be the supreme law of the land. . . ." (Article 6)

NO CONSTITUTIONAL SUPREMACY

If there were no constitutional supremacy, there would probably be chaos in the nation.

If the people do not provide the life-giving properties that permit the United States Constitution to live, to grow, to have strength, to resist the termites and insects, and to stand up under storms and other enemies of constitutional government, social, political, and economic chaos will result.

MACHINERY OF GOVERNMENT

DUAL FORM OF GOVERNMENT

"The United States shall guarantee to every state in this union a republican form of government." (Article 4, Section 4)

NO DUAL FORM OF GOVERNMENT

There are many restrictions on the federal government, among which are the first ten amendments — and numerous clauses throughout the United States Constitution.

"The powers not delegated to the United States by the Constitution . . . are reserved . . . to the people." (Amendment 10)

Legislative powers are limited by enumeration. (Article 1, Section 8)

They are limited by the statements of what the Congress cannot do. (Article 1, Section 9)

EXALTED JUDICIARY

Few other nations have a department that may judge the legality of a law made by the legislature.

The judges of the Supreme Court are students of the Constitution, the basic law of the land. If the people doubt that a law is constitutional, the law can be taken to the Supreme Court. If the Court decides that the law is contrary to the principles of the Constitution, the law is dead. Yours is a government of laws, not of men.

NO EXALTED JUDICIARY

If the constitutionality of the laws that go into the machinery of your government could not be tested and checked by the Supreme Court, your government would soon break down. Forty-eight states could pass forty-eight different kinds of legislation; the Congress could make itself all-powerful, or the President could seize powers and make himself a dictator.

Although the Constitution does not state in exact words that the Supreme Court has the power to declare acts of Congress unconstitutional, the Court has for over a century assumed that power. Custom has made this power as strong as if it actually were provided for by an article of the Constitution.

Commandments of Liberty

Charters of Freedom

FREEDOMS—CIVIL AND POLITICAL

The first great Charter of Freedom, the Ten Commandments, established the right of choice and responsibility for that choice. The United States Bill of Rights, another "Ten Commandments," again establishes your right of choice and your responsibility for that choice.

Men do not break these laws; these laws, if violated and ignored, break men.

NO FREEDOMS—CIVIL AND POLITICAL

Your basic civil and political freedoms are stated in the United States Constitution, especially in the first ten amendments — the "Bill of Rights," Amendments 13, 14, and 15, and in numerous other clauses preventing the state and federal governments from denying you your rights and liberties.

BIG PEOPLE AND LITTLE GOVERNMENT

GOVERNMENT OF LIMITED POWERS

Big People and Little Government is the way the colonists wanted it. In a republic, the people must ever be alert or the balance can change to big government and little people. When governmental powers are unlimited, freedom disappears.

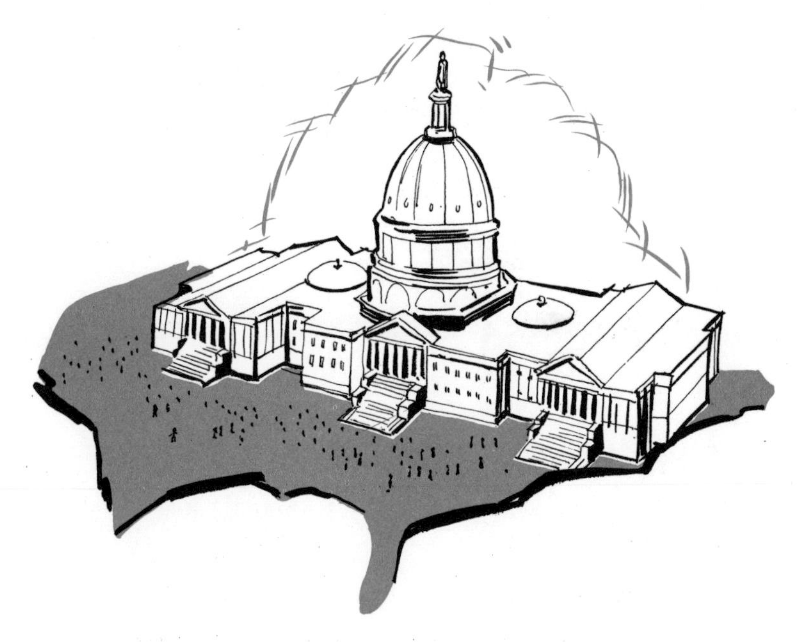

BIG GOVERNMENT AND LITTLE PEOPLE

NO GOVERNMENT OF LIMITED POWERS

The first ten amendments — especially 9 and 10 — and many other clauses throughout the United States Constitution limit the government's power. Your government, unlike some, possesses *only* those powers the people have given it, or choose to give it. Your Constitution gives you nothing; you already own those powers. The Constitution guarantees your rights.

Your Ship of State

Your Ships of States

A REPUBLICAN FORM OF GOVERNMENT

Watch for these three parts to a republican form of government:

1. People alone have power to create, operate, and alter their government.
2. The representatives of the people make the laws.
3. A written constitution usually sets forth the *laws.*

"The United States shall guarantee to every state in this union a republican form of government. . . ." (Article 4, Section 4)

"The right of citizens of the United States to vote shall not be denied or abridged by the United States or by any state on account of race, color, or previous condition of servitude . . . [or] on account of sex." (Amendments 15 and 19)

World's most powerful political force

If choice is lost

NO REPUBLICAN FORM OF GOVERNMENT

The heart of a republican form of government may be summarized in one word: *choice*. The opposite is true of Dictator*ship*. As people fail to exercise their choice by voting, *ice* forms, and the word becomes cho<u>ice</u>!

Thomas Jefferson:

"A bill of rights is what the people are entitled to against every government on earth, general or particular, and what no just government should refuse or rest on inference."

INSTRUMENTS OF FREEDOM
vs.
INSTRUMENTS OF TYRANNY

TWENTY-FIVE GUARANTEES

You Are Guaranteed—

THE WRIT OF HABEAS CORPUS

"The privilege of the writ of habeas corpus . . ." means that a person who has been arrested can make his jailer take him to a judge. Those who have arrested the man must convince the judge that the prisoner has committed a crime; otherwise the prisoner must be freed.

The words "habeas corpus" are Latin words that mean, "You may have the body."

NO WRIT OF HABEAS CORPUS

Having destroyed the writ, the dictator can keep his religious, political, financial, and personal enemies in prison indefinitely without telling them why they are in jail, and without giving them a hearing or a trial.

"The privilege of the writ of habeas corpus shall not be suspended, unless when in cases of rebellion or invasion the public safety may require it." (Article 1, Section 9)

You Are Guaranteed—

PROTECTION AGAINST BILLS OF ATTAINDER

Before you can be convicted of a crime, you must be found guilty in and by a court of law, not by an act of a legislature or other public body.

A law that inflicts punishment without giving the accused person a trial in a court of law is called a bill of attainder. Such a law is specifically forbidden by the Constitution.

NO PROTECTION AGAINST BILLS OF ATTAINDER

This method of conviction is an old favorite of tyrants. Conviction by legislation has long been an effective way of silencing the opposition temporarily or permanently. No gathering of evidence, no listening to the defense, no long-drawn-out trials are necessary. The one "attainted" or convicted:

1. Loses all his real and personal property.
2. Can neither receive property, nor pass it on to his children or to others.
3. Cannot sue, or testify in any court.
4. Cannot claim any legal protection or rights.

"No bill of attainder . . . shall be passed." (Article 1, Section 9)

You Are Guaranteed—

PROTECTION AGAINST EX POST FACTO LAWS

When a law is passed making an act a crime, the law becomes effective the day it is passed or at a later date. The law cannot be made to take effect before the date of its passage.

Ex post facto laws include:

1. "Every law that makes an action done before the passing of the law, and which was innocent when done, criminal, and punishes such action.
2. "Every law that aggravates a crime, or makes it greater than it was when committed.
3. "Every law that changes the punishment, and inflicts a greater punishment than the law annexed to the crime when committed.
4. "Every law that alters the legal rules of evidence, and receives less or different testimony than the law required at the time of commission of the offense in order to convict the offender." — Samuel Chase

NO PROTECTION AGAINST EX POST FACTO LAWS

"No . . . ex post facto law shall be passed." (Article 1, Section 9)

You Are Guaranteed—

EQUALITY BEFORE THE LAW; NO TITLES OF NOBILITY

To be a *Lady* or *Gentleman* in some countries, one must have inherited the right to be so classified. In the United States anyone who wishes may be a lady or a gentleman.

True nobility, the nobility of spirit, of achievement, of character, is a status anyone may achieve.

COULD THIS HAPPEN HERE?

NO EQUALITY BEFORE THE LAW; TITLES OF NOBILITY

You must keep alert to any attempt on the part of your Congress, state legislature, city council, or other body to create a privileged class.

"The citizens of each state shall be entitled to all privileges and immunities of citizens in the several states." (Article 4, Section 2)

"No title of nobility shall be granted by the United States. . . ." (Article 1, Section 9)

"No state shall . . . deny to any person within its jurisdiction the equal protection of the laws." (Amendment 14)

You Are Guaranteed—

FREEDOM OF RELIGION, SPEECH, PRESS, ASSEMBLY, PETITION

These five freedoms — freedom of religion, freedom of speech, freedom of the press, freedom to assemble peaceably, freedom to petition for redress of grievances — are guarantees against the national government's encroachment on your basic individual rights. None of these rights is absolute. For instance, you may not break a criminal law in the name of religion; you may not through the freedom of the press advocate rebellion; you may not through the freedom of speech encourage disobedience to law; your peaceful assembly may not block city streets.

These five freedoms, which are not enjoyed by all peoples in all other nations, are necessary to you. With these freedoms you can keep your government a government of the people.

NO FREEDOM OF RELIGION, SPEECH, PRESS, ASSEMBLY, PETITION

No Freedom of Religion

This is happening in some places in the world today. Guard well your religious freedom! Let neither friend nor foe infringe on your right to worship God as you desire.

No Freedom of Speech

If people cannot talk, they cannot exchange ideas and state their opinions. Dictators prefer this way.

Continued on page 42

No Freedom of Press

No better method exists of commending good government and of exposing graft and fraud in bad government than a free press. Without it, the people are almost powerless.

"Congress shall make no law respecting . . . religion, . . . abridging the freedom of speech, or of the press; or the right . . . peaceably to assemble, and to petition. . . ." (Amendment 1)

No Freedom of Assembly

By preventing meetings, a dictator can check what people might be doing to overthrow his rule. It is difficult

to organize a revolution or resistance if people cannot gather to talk over their plans.

No Freedom of Petition

You, the average citizen, own no radio or television station. You own no newspaper or magazine. You make few speeches. You are probably too far from your legislature or congress to call personally.

If you did not have the right to petition your government, you could not present your case in person to the governing body. To express even the idea that something could be done better, or that people are being injured by the government, could be sufficient reason for your enslavement or death.

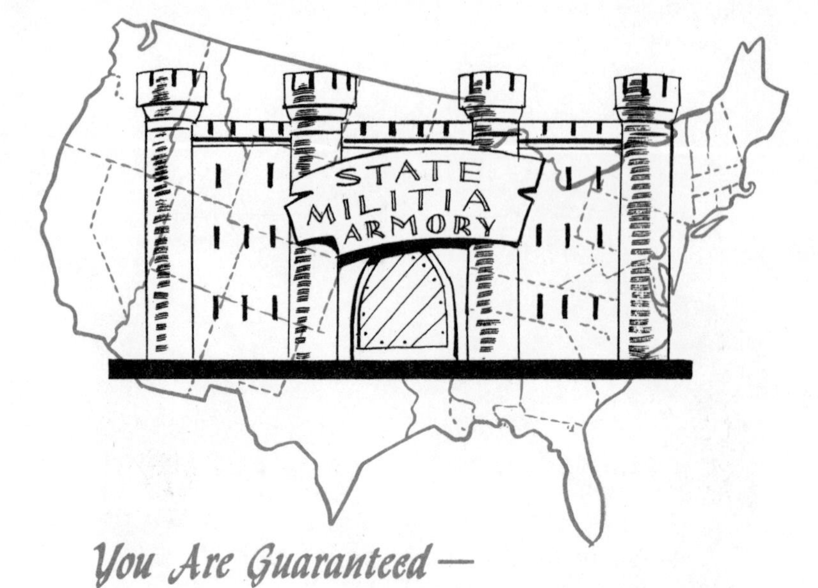

You Are Guaranteed—

THE RIGHT TO KEEP AND BEAR ARMS

The people who demanded the first ten amendments to your Constitution felt that a well regulated militia was necessary to the security of a free state, and that the people had the right to keep and bear arms. The arms referred to are those of the soldier; both the state and the federal governments may restrict the bearing of arms for private use.

It was the purpose of this guarantee to place the defense of the state in the hands of the militia to be drawn from the people, rather than in a standing army.

In times of war, the National Guard may become a part of the United States Army. In such cases state guards are often formed for home protection.

NO RIGHT TO KEEP AND BEAR ARMS

So long as you keep your right to have a state militia or National Guard and to regulate who shall carry arms and under what conditions, dictators will find it difficult to seize your state or national government. In times of peace, the state governor is the head of the militia.

". . . the right . . . to keep and bear arms, shall not be infringed." (Amendment 2)

You Are Guaranteed—

PROTECTION AGAINST QUARTERING OF TROOPS

Your home is sacred to you and is for your own use. The government may not in time of peace quarter troops in it without your permission; soldiers may be put in your home in time of war only in a manner to be prescribed by law.

NO PROTECTION AGAINST QUARTERING OF TROOPS

When parliaments or legislatures refused to appropriate money to pay for the room and board of soldiers, kings and tyrants used to force the people to open their homes and provide meals and shelter for the soldiers. Sometimes the kings would levy taxes on a local community to pay for the expenses of the soldiers camped nearby.

"No soldier shall, in time of peace, be quartered in any house, without the consent of the owner. . . ." (Amendment 3)

You Are Guaranteed—

PROTECTION AGAINST UNREASONABLE SEARCH AND SEIZURE

You are entitled to live free from the worry that officers may enter your home at will or stop you or your family and search you when they please. Only with a properly issued search warrant may an officer demand admittance to your home or search your person. The warrant can be issued only upon probable cause, supported by oath. The warrant must describe the place to be searched and the persons or things to be seized.

The word "unreasonable" suggests that there are occasions on which *searches* and *seizures* are reasonable, even though the officer has no warrant. Thus, an officer may search a vehicle that can be moved away to permit the disposal of evidence while the officer is getting a warrant. An officer may enter a house if he has reason to believe that someone is hiding there who has broken the peace or has committed a felony.

NO PROTECTION AGAINST UNREASONABLE SEARCH AND SEIZURE

If you were subject to unreasonable search, it would be easy for someone to "plant" evidence on you. You could be stopped, molested, embarrassed, and even arrested times without number. Such actions might make you feel so insecure that your health would be ruined and you would lose your job.

If your home were not protected from search without a search warrant, your home could be entered and upset repeatedly, evidence could be "planted," and papers and other things could be seized.

Always demand to see a search warrant if anyone insists on entering your home.

"The right of the people to be secure . . . against unreasonable searches and seizures, shall not be violated. . . ." (Amendment 4)

THE ART OF FREEDOM

You Are Guaranteed—

THE RIGHT TO LIFE, LIBERTY, AND PROPERTY

The art of freedom has been thousands of years in developing. Among the many masterpieces are the following:

1. You are guaranteed that before you can be brought to trial by the federal government for a capital or otherwise infamous crime you must be charged with the crime before a grand jury that usually consists of from 12 to 23 persons. The evidence against you, the accused, is presented by a district attorney. If the jury finds there is not enough evidence to support the accusation, you are

Continued on page 52

NO RIGHT TO LIFE, LIBERTY, AND PROPERTY

A. No Grand Jury Indictment

If there were no indictment by the grand jury, you could be placed on trial without having your fellow citizens review the case against you.

Remember that though the grand jury procedure seems slow and cumbersome, it is insurance for you, and millions like you, that you will not be held for trial unless your fellow citizens agree that you should be.

B. No Right to Be Confronted by Your Accusers

C. No Subpoena Power for Your Witnesses

The power of subpoena is a valuable weapon which you must always keep sharp and ready for your defense.

D. No Counsel

1. Right to Grand Jury Indictment

"No person shall be held to answer for a capital, or otherwise infamous crime, unless on a presentment or indictment of a grand jury. . . ." (Amendment 5)

Continued on page 53

dismissed; if the jury thinks the evidence is sufficient to show that you were involved in the crime, the jury will issue a true indictment, or a writ, holding you for trial.

Indictment by a grand jury does not apply to members of the armed forces or the militia when in actual service in time of war or public danger.

2. At the trial, you and your attorney have the right to see, to hear, and to question all witnesses against you.

3. You, the accused, have the right to compel witnesses who can tell your side of the case to appear and to testify. Witnesses may be brought to court by a subpoena, which is an official summons. "Subpoena" comes from the Latin meaning "under punishment." A person who does not obey the summons may be punished.

4. If you, the accused, cannot afford a lawyer, the judge will appoint one for you; therefore, you are assured at least that you will not convict yourself because of ignorance of your rights.

2. Right to Face Your Accuser

"In all criminal prosecutions, the accused shall enjoy the right . . . to be confronted with the witness against him." (Amendment 6)

3. Right to Subpoena

"In all criminal prosecutions, the accused shall enjoy the right . . . to have compulsory process for obtaining witness. . . ." (Amendment 6)

4. Right to Counsel

"In all criminal prosecutions, the accused shall enjoy the right . . . to have the assistance of counsel. . . ." (Amendment 6)

You Are Guaranteed—

A SPEEDY AND PUBLIC TRIAL AT PLACE OF CRIME

A speedy trial means that the trial must be held within a reasonable time. You, the accused, must have time to prepare for your defense; you may not be held indefinitely before your case is tried.

Public trial means that your trial must be held openly, not secretly.

The jury is composed of fellow citizens who are not to favor you or your accusers. They are sworn to give their true decision based on the evidence presented for and against you. You must be tried in the state in which the crime was committed.

These are major guarantees without which no one, innocent or guilty, would be safe. Man struggled for hundreds of years to arrive at this point in his dealings with the law.

NO SPEEDY AND PUBLIC TRIAL AT PLACE OF CRIME

Were it not for the provision in your Constitution stating the rights of a person accused of a crime, you could be secretly arrested, secretly taken away, and secretly held a prisoner, uninformed about the reason for your arrest. If you were tried, you would have only witnesses against you, none for you. Your jury could be a group of people selected for the sole purpose of convicting you.

Guard well the guaranteed rights of the accused.

"In all criminal prosecutions, the accused shall enjoy the right to a speedy and public trial. . . ." (Amendment 6)

You Are Guaranteed—

PROTECTION AGAINST DOUBLE JEOPARDY

No person shall be subject for the same offense to be twice put in jeopardy of life or limb. Once you have been tried and a verdict has been reached, guilty or not guilty, you cannot be tried again for the same offense, even though evidence were later found that proved your guilt or might have brought about a more severe penalty.

The phrase "in jeopardy of life or limb" comes from the days when a person could be punished by cutting off his head, his arm, or his leg.

NO PROTECTION AGAINST DOUBLE JEOPARDY

This cannot happen to you because your constitution says:

". . . nor shall any person be subject for the same offense to be twice put in jeopardy. . . ." (Amendment 5)

You Are Guaranteed—

PROTECTION AGAINST SELF-INCRIMINATION

The Fifth Amendment was written to protect you when you are accused of committing a crime. You have a right to be thought innocent until you are found to be guilty. The government must produce the evidence to prove your guilt. You cannot be forced to testify against yourself and thus trap yourself into your own conviction.

NO PROTECTION AGAINST SELF-INCRIMINATION

". . . nor shall be compelled in any criminal case to be a witness against himself. . . ." (Amendment 5)

You Are Guaranteed—

PROTECTION AGAINST CRUEL AND UNUSUAL PUNISHMENT AND EXCESSIVE BAIL

The punishment and the size of the bail must be no greater than the seriousness of the crime. If the bail and the fines are excessive and the punishment unreasonable, you have the right to appeal.

NO PROTECTION AGAINST CRUEL AND UNUSUAL PUNISHMENT AND EXCESSIVE BAIL

"Excessive bail shall not be required, nor excessive fines imposed, nor cruel and unusual punishments inflicted." (Amendment 8)

You Are Guaranteed—

JUST COMPENSATION FOR PRIVATE PROPERTY TAKEN FOR PUBLIC USE

The government has the right to take any private property for public use by paying the owner a fair price.

If the owner is dissatisfied with the price, he has the right to present to a court or administrative board facts to try to prove that his property is more valuable.

NO JUST COMPENSATION FOR PRIVATE PROPERTY TAKEN FOR PUBLIC USE

". . . nor shall private property be taken for public use, without just compensation." (Amendment 5)

You Are Guaranteed—

RIGHT TO TRIAL BY JURY IN CIVIL CASES

Civil law and criminal law differ. Civil law relates to your private rights as an individual in your community, and to legal proceedings in connection with those rights. Criminal law relates to crime or its punishment.

Civil cases usually result from disagreements between individuals. These disagreements ordinarily arise from differences about rights and duties each owes the other.

If a civil suit is tried in a federal court, those involved in the suit may have a jury if they desire and if the case involves more than $20. Should the parties not wish a jury, they may agree to do without one.

NO RIGHT TO TRIAL BY JURY IN CIVIL CASES

If citizens were denied a trial by jury in civil cases, corrupt officials could bring people to trial and financial ruin. Because of your right to a jury trial, your fellow citizens may hear your case and make a decision.

"In suits at common law, where the value in controversy shall exceed twenty dollars, the right of trial by jury shall be preserved. . . ." (Amendment 7)

You Are Guaranteed—

DUE PROCESS OF LAW

No two words in your Constitution are more important than *due process*. The first word, "due," relates to the conduct of your trial, or your procedural rights: that you must be duly notified; that you must be given a fair and proper trial in an authorized court; that you may have an attorney for your defense; that you may face your accusers; that you may secure evidence by aid of the law.

The second word, "process," relates to the fairness of the law. If you feel that a law of the city, county, state, or Congress is unjust, you may take your case to the Supreme Court for its decision.

The Fifth and the Fourteenth Amendments protect you from unjust laws.

"No trial"

NO DUE PROCESS OF LAW

Without the "due process" clause this could happen to *you*.

". . . nor shall any person . . . be deprived of life, liberty, or property, without due process of law." (Amendment 5 and Amendment 14, Section 1)

You Are Guaranteed—

SANCTITY OF CONTRACTS

Business can flow smoothly and regularly because you are guaranteed that the terms of contracts honestly, sincerely, and legally made cannot be weakened by any state law. The phrase "legally made" means that no contract can be enforced if it is contrary to law. The restriction concerning impairment of contract also applies to the federal government.

NO SANCTITY OF CONTRACTS

Chaos and utter ruin would result to all business and to your community if contracts were not firm and binding. If governments could pass laws cancelling contracts that were honestly and sincerely made, there would be no guarantee that anyone would do what he agreed to do.

"No state shall . . . pass any . . . law impairing obligation of contracts. . . ." (Article 1, Section 10)

You Are Guaranteed—

EQUAL PROTECTION OF THE LAWS

Originally, "equal protection under the law" was intended to prevent the passing of laws denying political and civil rights to the Negro. Its meaning has since been extended to include all persons — citizens and aliens.

NO EQUAL PROTECTION OF THE LAWS

"No state shall . . . deny to any person within its jurisdiction the equal protection of the laws." (Amendment 14, Section 1)

You Are Guaranteed—

REPUBLICAN FORM OF GOVERNMENT IN YOUR STATE

The Constitution guarantees every state, and therefore every citizen, a REPUBLICAN FORM OF GOVERNMENT. A republican form of government is a representative type of government in which you, the voter, are the boss, for if your representatives do not do what the majority wish, the majority may change those representatives.

NO REPUBLICAN FORM OF GOVERNMENT IN YOUR STATE

Under the Constitution, the federal government guarantees to every state a republican form of government. This guarantee was made to prevent the establishment of any other form of government, such as a monarchy, within the nation. The term "republican" is nowhere explained, but it means government by elected representatives. The people do not lose all their power of making direct legislation, for in many states the people have the initiative and the referendum. The makers of the Constitution wanted to prevent any group from seizing a state government and setting up a dictatorship in that state.

"The United States shall guarantee to every state . . . a republican form of government. . . ." (Article 4, Section 4)

You Are Guaranteed—

PROTECTION AGAINST SLAVERY AND INVOLUNTARY SERVITUDE

You cannot be held in slavery. You cannot be kept in involuntary servitude except as punishment for a crime of which you have been duly convicted.

NO PROTECTION AGAINST SLAVERY AND INVOLUNTARY SERVITUDE

This once happened! Slavery cannot happen as long as you keep your Constitution in force.

"Neither slavery nor involuntary servitude . . . shall exist within the United States. . . ." (Amendment 13, Section 1)

You Are Guaranteed—

PROTECTION AGAINST DISCRIMINATION OF ONE STATE AGAINST THE CITIZENS OF ANOTHER

The citizens of each state shall be entitled to all the privileges and immunities of citizens in the several states. This provision makes it possible for you to move freely from one state to another and to settle where you will. You are assured that you will have the same civil rights — to own property, to engage in a business, to enjoy all the privileges and immunities and the same protection under the law — as any citizen in the state. In other words, if you move from Vermont into California, you are guaranteed such rights as the people in California have; you are not guaranteed the rights you enjoyed in Vermont.

NO PROTECTION AGAINST DISCRIMINATION OF ONE STATE AGAINST THE CITIZENS OF ANOTHER

It would be possible for a state to charge an admittance and an exit fee for entering and leaving the state.

What confusion and unfair treatment could result if one state could ignore the rights of citizens from other states! Such restrictions would destroy the unity of the nation. Such restrictions would destroy free trade. Such restrictions would prevent unlimited travel.

"The citizens of each state shall be entitled to all privileges and immunities of citizens in the several states." (Article 4, Section 2)

YOU

You Are Guaranteed—

PROTECTION AGAINST RELIGIOUS TESTS FOR HOLDING PUBLIC OFFICE

If you can meet the requirements for officeholders, you are eligible for office regardless of your religion.

NO PROTECTION AGAINST RELIGIOUS TESTS FOR HOLDING PUBLIC OFFICE

If a religious test could be required of candidates for public office, a dictator could create his own religion and his own test. By this means he could select all the candidates for public office and public trust.

". . . No religious test shall ever be required as a qualification to any office or public trust under the United States." (Article 6, Clause 3)

You Are Guaranteed—

ENTRANCE INTO AND EXIT FROM STATES

The right freely to enter or to leave a state is important. This right has probably done more to encourage the expansion of our territory, the development of our national resources, the unification of our republic, than any other right. Persons going from one state to another by any form of transportation, even by walking, are considered a part of interstate commerce over which Congress, not the states, has control. True, the right is not absolute, for the states through their policing power can impose reasonable regulations that restrict free coming and going in order to protect health and property. For example, the state can deny you the right to bring in property — such as a truckload of TNT — unless you comply with safety rules.

NO ENTRANCE INTO AND EXIT FROM STATES

"The citizens of each state shall be entitled to all privileges and immunities of citizens in the several states." (Article 4, Section 2)

You Are Guaranteed—

PROTECTION FROM FOREIGN INVASION AND DOMESTIC UPRISING

The strength of one state is the strength of all the states. Should a group of people attempt to take over your state by force or violence, or should a foreign army try to invade your state, the entire strength of the nation is pledged to protect you.

NO PROTECTION FROM FOREIGN INVASION AND DOMESTIC UPRISING

If the government did not guarantee protection against invasion and aid in the stopping of domestic disorders, a foreign enemy could invade and capture state after state, for no state by itself could maintain an effective resistance. A state government could be overthrown by domestic violence. Interstate commerce could be ruined. People in other states might suffer. All civil rights, national and local, could be destroyed.

"The United States . . . shall protect each of them [the states] against invasion; and . . . against domestic violence." (Article 4, Section 4)

You Are Guaranteed—

PROTECTION OF THE RIGHT TO VOTE

The Fifteenth and Nineteenth Amendments forbid the United States or a state to restrict or deny the right of citizens of the United States to vote on account of race, color, or previous condition of servitude, or sex. The Constitution does not guarantee anyone the right to vote. The amendments merely state certain conditions that cannot be used to deny a citizen the privilege of voting. The state sets forth the qualifications its citizens must meet if they wish to exercise the privilege of voting. These qualifications may vary from state to state.

NO PROTECTION OF THE RIGHT TO VOTE

The more limited the right to vote, the less voice the people have in the government. The government ceases to be the servant of the people — the people become the servants of the government.

"The right of citizens of the United States to vote shall not be denied or abridged by the United States or by any state on account of race, color, or previous condition of servitude . . . [or] on account of sex." (Amendments 15 and 19)

INSTRUMENTS OF A REPUBLIC

HOW TO PLAY YOUR PART

LIVE WIRES

Apart from the people, its source of power, the Constitution is as forceless as an idle electric generator with no energy to turn it. However, when connected with the stream of co-operative public support, this great Constitution enables a production of power unequalled in all the history of man's struggle to govern himself.

Power is useless until it is put to work in homes, factories, industries, schools, churches, hospitals, offices, and transportation. As electric power must be applied, so must your Constitution be applied. The power made possible by your Constitution must be conducted, channeled, wired, or sent to locations where it is to be used.

There are many "wires" by which the current generated by the Constitution is taken to every citizen of this land. One such wire goes to the mighty electric organ on which Uncle Sam plays our unfinished symphony — "Sweet Freedom's Song."

Each of these wires is as important for the United States as an instrument is to an orchestra; as important as a stop is to an organ. These "factors of freedom" that have helped to develop your country were made possible by your Constitution. Only as you put them to work does your Constitution have meaning for you.

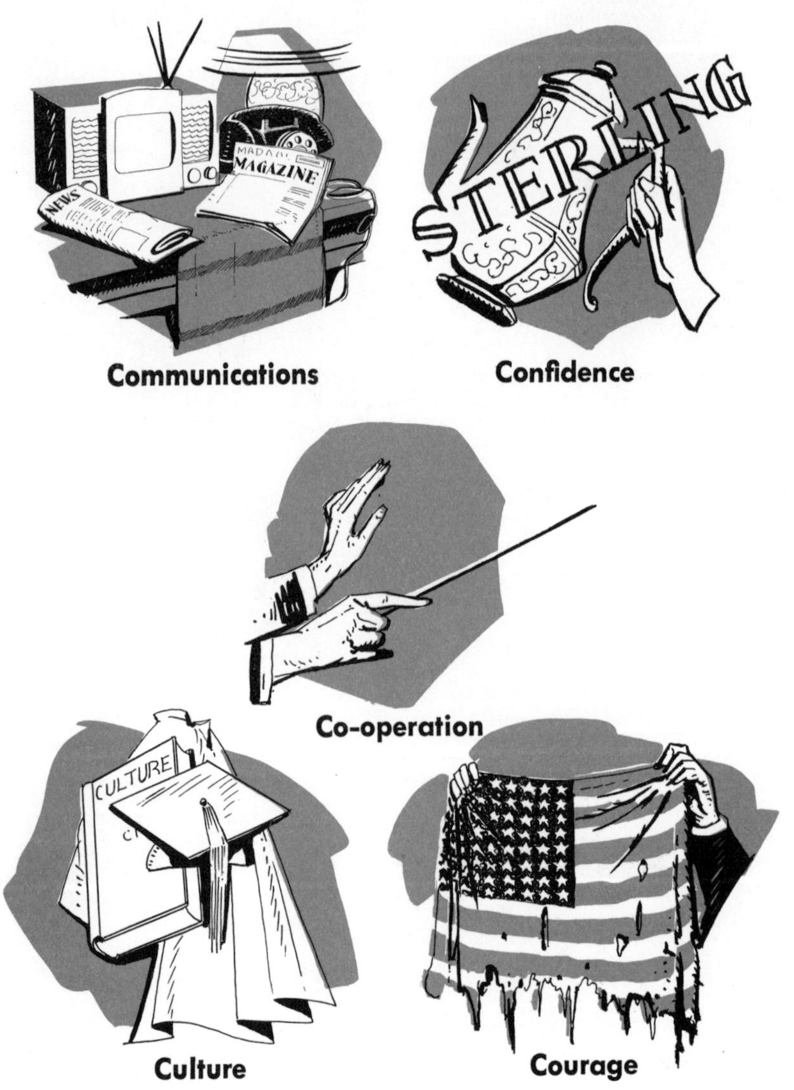

Communications

Confidence

Co-operation

Culture

Courage

Determination

Education

Faith

Family

Generosity

Genius of American People

Not the least important factor in your nation's success is the geniUS (geni United States) of the American people to solve internal and external problems. This is possible under your type of government only when you assume your full share of public duty.

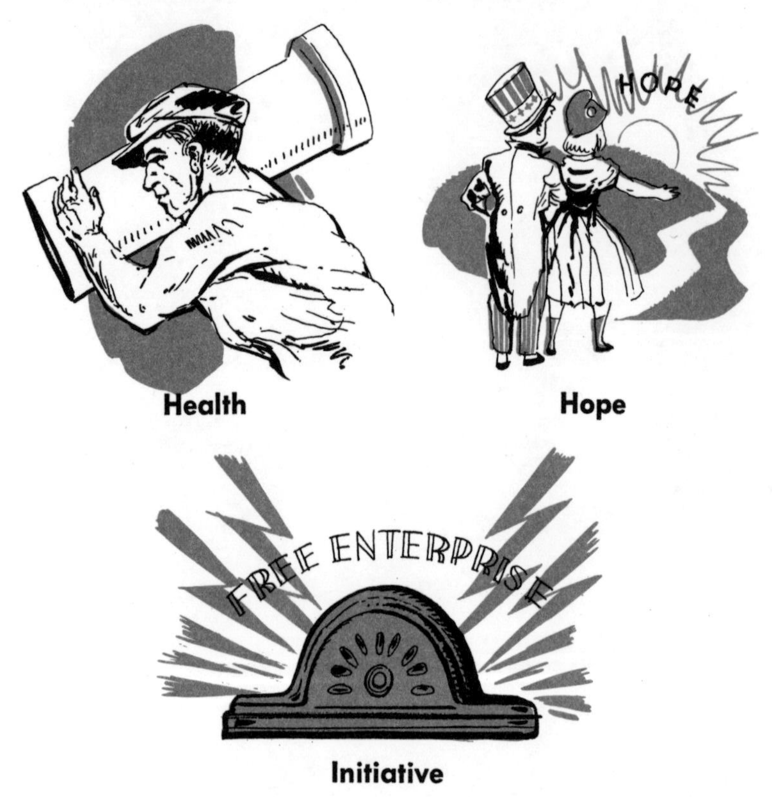

Health

Hope

Initiative

Our American system of free enterprise is no mere accident. It is powered by your Constitution, which guarantees to every citizen the right to own personal and real property.

Initiative is encouraged by patents and copyrights, which are protected under your Constitution. The inventiveness and the "know-how" of our people are an outgrowth of your type of government.

"The Congress shall have power . . . to promote the progress of science and useful arts, by securing for limited times to authors and inventors the exclusive right to their respective writings and discoveries. . . ." (Article 1, Section 8)

Labor

Labor is the effective use of the quality and quantity of man's muscular and mental energy. A man may choose his own work; bargain with his employer.

Leadership

Leadership in society, religion, business, culture, and industry is one of your natural assets.

Loyalty

Management

Management is the intelligent direction of skills and human energy: The better the direction, the better the results for all.

"ONE NATION UNDER GOD-
INDIVISIBLE - WITH
LIBERTY AND JUSTICE
FOR ALL"

Mutual Respect

Resources

Responsibility

Rewards

From the intelligent use of tools you get rewards or profits. The better use you make of your tools of production, the higher the standard of living for all.

Savings

Savings come from self-denial. From your savings you get the tools with which to produce, to satisfy your needs, to meet emergencies, to provide for the future.

Skillfulness **Spirituality**

Tools of Production

Because your Constitution guarantees the right to property, every citizen may own some of the tools of production. His tools may be a hammer, a delivery truck, stock in a corporation, or government bonds.

Tools come from the savings of people.

HOW YOU "LET FREEDOM RING"

You can "let freedom ring" by playing your part in this great American orchestra, an orchestra with all the "instruments" necessary and 165 million musicians to play them.

Whether the music will be sweet, tuneful, and harmonious, or sour, discordant, and unpleasant depends upon you and what you do about your citizenship.

As one off-key musician can spoil a concert, so one off-key citizen can spoil a community.

There are certain definite things you can *do* to help make this a better country.

AMENDING PROCESS

The Constitution provides for making orderly adjust-

ments to meet economic, political, and social changes. No violence is necessary to change your Constitution.

BALANCES AND CHECKS

Write your Congressman *not* to surrender to the President the powers that *you*, the people, have assigned to Congress.

Urge your President to appoint to the Supreme Court only the very highest type of men. Urge the President not to attempt to assume powers *you* did not assign to him in the Constitution.

Vote always, and vote intelligently.

CONSTITUTIONAL SUPREMACY

Help recall local or state judges and encourage the impeachment of federal judges and other officials who refuse to recognize the supremacy of the United States Constitution.

Support only those organizations that uphold the basic principles in the Constitution. Join only those groups that you know are loyal to constitutional government.

If the roots of your United States Constitution are infected by poison, the tree will weaken and finally fall. If this happens, your liberties will be gone.

DUAL FORM OF GOVERNMENT

Talk to your legislators.

Let your Congressmen know you don't want either your state or your federal government to interfere with the authority given to the other by the Constitution.

Vote for those proposals and people who will help carry out your will.

Phone your neighbors to vote.

Support the press and radio that support your beliefs.

EXALTED JUDICIARY

Vote out of office any officials who would weaken the powers *you* have vested in your Supreme Court. Urge the impeachment of any Supreme Court justice who violates his oath of office or brings disgrace to the high post he holds.

FREEDOMS — THE GREATEST POWER ON EARTH

FREEDOMS—CIVIL AND POLITICAL

Act definitely and swiftly against any official, public or private, who does anything that may take away the civil and political freedoms set up for you and given to you in trust. If you let any of your freedoms lapse, they may all disappear.

GOVERNMENT OF LIMITED POWERS

Be sharp! Keep alert! Always be looking and watching for any attempt on the part of any branch of your government to assume powers not given to it.

Never let the shadow of your government become longer than the shadow of you, the people. If you see this danger coming:

Get time on radio and television and before clubs to warn your friends to act NOW. Tomorrow may be too late.

A REPUBLICAN FORM OF GOVERNMENT

No matter how powerful, the federal government cannot guarantee to your state a republican form of government unless you do your part. Governments are instruments in the hands of men. If your government is

"... TO EVERY STATE IN THE UNION A REPRESENTATIVE FORM OF GOVERNMENT"

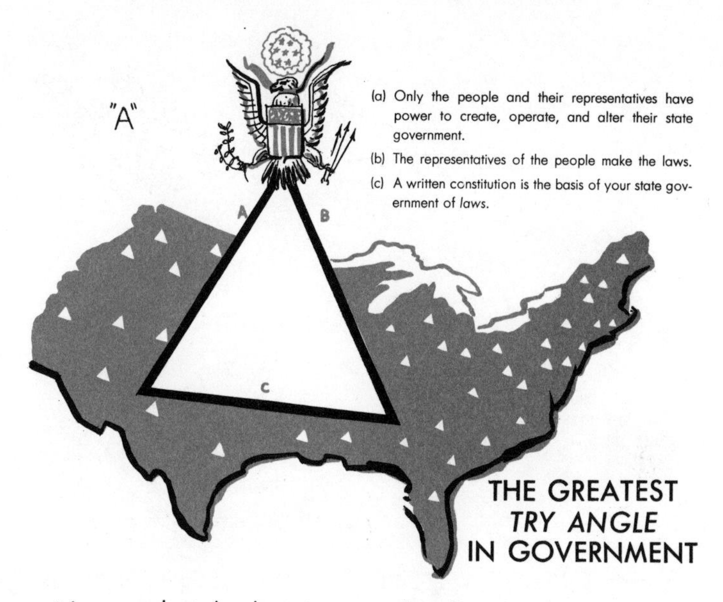

not in your hands, then it is in other hands. Whose are those hands?

If you neglect your ballot box, others can alter and operate your government. Unless you keep alert, you may lose your right of choice.

If you neglect to send good representatives to your Congress, state legislature, county and city governments, to school boards and other bodies, you are surrendering your power.

ASLEEP ON HIS THRONE   **WHILE THE VOTER SLEPT**

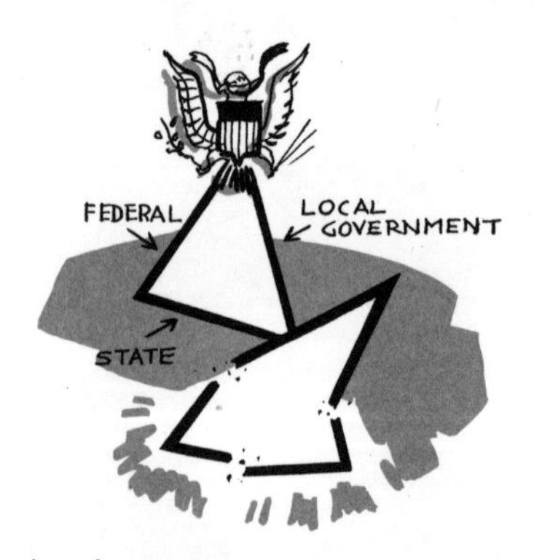

Like your federal government, your state and local governments are governments of *LAWS* and not of *MEN*. Government can scarcely be one of laws if there is no basic principle upon which the other laws rest. Remove one side of the TRY ANGLE and your pedestal falls.

Without state constitutions and county and city charters, the government TRY ANGLE is incomplete. It can't stand. "Eternal vigilance" has always been and is now "the price of liberty."

Guard constitutional government with your life. Neglect it, and you may lose it. Protect it, and it will protect you.

CONSTITUTION OF THE UNITED STATES

CONSTITUTION OF THE UNITED STATES

*We the people of the United States, in order to form a more perfect union, establish justice, insure domestic tranquility, provide for the common defence, promote the general welfare, and secure the blessings of liberty to ourselves and our posterity, do ordain and establish this Constitution for the United States of America.**

ARTICLE I.

Section 1. All legislative powers herein granted shall be vested in a Congress of the United States, which shall consist of a Senate and House of Representatives.

Section 2. *The House of Representatives shall* be composed of members *chosen every second year* by the people of the several states, and the electors in each state shall have the qualifications requisite for electors of the most numerous branch of the state legislature.

No person shall be a Representative who shall not have attained to the age of twenty-five years, and been seven years a citizen of the United States, and who shall not, when elected, be an inhabitant of that state in which he shall be chosen.

Representatives and direct taxes shall be apportioned among the several states which may be included within this union, according to their respective numbers, ~~which shall be determined by adding to the whole number of free persons, including those bound to service for a term of years~~, and excluding Indians not taxed, ~~three fifths of all other persons~~.[1] The actual enumeration shall be made within three years after the first meeting of the Congress of the United States, and within every subsequent term of ten years, in such manner as they shall by law direct. The number of Representatives shall not exceed one for every thirty thousand, but each state shall have at least one Representative; and until such enumeration shall be made, the State of New Hampshire shall be entitled to choose three, Massachusetts eight, Rhode Island and Providence Plantations one, Connecticut five, New York six, New Jersey four, Pennsylvania eight, Delaware one, Maryland six, Virginia ten,

**Italics* indicate those passages cited earlier in this book.

[1]See 14th Amendment.

North Carolina five, South Carolina five, and Georgia three.

When vacancies happen in the representation from any state, the executive authority thereof shall issue writs of election to fill such vacancies.

The House of Representatives shall choose their speaker and other officers; and *shall have the sole power of impeachment.*

Section 3. The Senate of the United States shall be composed of two Senators from each state, ~~chosen by the legislature thereof~~,[2] for six years; and each Senator shall have one vote.

Immediately after they shall be assembled in consequence of the first election, they shall be divided as equally as may be into three classes. The seats of the Senators of the first class shall be vacated at the expiration of the second year, of the second class at the expiration of the fourth year, and of the third class at the expiration of the sixth year, so that one third may be chosen every second year; ~~and if vacancies happen by resignation, or otherwise, during the recess of the legislature of any state, the executive thereof may make temporary appointments until the next meeting of the legislature, which shall then fill such vacancies.~~[3]

No person shall be a Senator who shall not have attained to the age of thirty years, and been nine years a citizen of the United States, and who shall not, when elected, be an inhabitant of that state for which he shall be chosen.

The Vice President of the United States shall be President of the Senate, but shall have no vote, unless they be equally divided.

The Senate shall choose their other officers, and also a President pro tempore, in the absence of the Vice President, or when he shall exercise the office of President of the United States.

The Senate shall have the sole power to try all impeachments. When sitting for that purpose, they shall be on oath or affirmation. When the President of the United States is tried, the Chief Justice shall preside: and no person shall be convicted without the concurrence of two thirds of the members present.

Judgment in cases of impeachment shall not extend further than to removal from office, and disqualification to hold and enjoy any office of honor, trust or profit under the United States: but the party

[2] See 17th Amendment.

[3] *Ibid.*

convicted shall nevertheless be liable and subject to indictment, trial, judgment and punishment, according to law.

Section 4. The times, places and manner of holding elections for Senators and Representatives shall be prescribed in each state by the legislature thereof; but the Congress may at any time by law make or alter such regulations, except as to the places of choosing Senators.

~~*The Congress shall assemble at least once in every year, and such meeting shall be on the first Monday in December, unless they shall by law appoint a different day.*~~[4]

Section 5. Each House shall be the judge of the elections, returns and qualifications of its own members, and a majority of each shall constitute a quorum to do business; but a smaller number may adjourn from day to day, and may be authorized to compel the attendance of absent members, in such manner, and under such penalties as each House may provide.

Each House may determine the rules of its proceedings, punish its members for disorderly behavior, and, with the concurrence of two thirds, expel a member.

Each House shall keep a journal of its proceedings, and from time to time publish the same, excepting such parts as may in their judgment require secrecy; and the yeas and nays of the members of either House on any question shall, at the desire of one fifth of those present, be entered on the journal.

Neither House, during the session of Congress, shall, without the consent of the other, adjourn for more than three days, nor to any other place than that in which the two Houses shall be sitting.

Section 6. The Senators and Representatives shall receive a compensation for their services, to be ascertained by law, and paid out of the Treasury of the United States. They shall in all cases, except treason, felony and breach of the peace, be privileged from arrest during their attendance at the session of their respective Houses, and in going to and returning from the same; and for any speech or debate in either House, they shall not be questioned in any other place.

No Senator or Representative shall, during the time for which he

[4]See 20th Amendment.

was elected, be appointed to any civil office under the authority of the United States, which shall have been created, or the emoluments whereof shall have been encreased during such time; and no person holding any office under the United States, shall be a member of either House during his continuance in office.

Section 7. *All bills for raising revenue shall originate in the House of Representatives;* but the Senate may propose or concur with amendments as on other bills.

Every bill which shall have passed the House of Representatives and the Senate, shall, before it become a law, be presented to the President of the United States; *if he approve he shall sign it, but if not he shall return it, with his objections* to that House in which it shall have originated, who shall enter the objections at large on their journal, and proceed to reconsider it. If after such reconsideration two thirds of that House shall agree to pass the bill, it shall be sent, together with the objections, to the other House, by which it shall likewise be reconsidered, and *if approved by two thirds* of that House, *it shall become a law*. But in all such cases the votes of both Houses shall be determined by yeas and nays, and the names of the persons voting for and against the bill shall be entered on the journal of each House respectively. If any bill shall not be returned by the President within ten days (Sundays excepted) after it shall have been presented to him, the same shall be a law, in like manner as if he had signed it, unless Congress by their adjournment prevent its return, in which case it shall not be a law.

Every order, resolution, or vote to which the concurrence of the Senate and House of Representatives may be necessary (except on a question of adjournment) shall be presented to the President of the United States; and before the same shall take effect, shall be approved by him, or being disapproved by him, shall be repassed by two thirds of the Senate and House of Representatives, according to the rules and limitations prescribed in the case of a bill.

Section 8. *The Congress shall have power* To lay and collect taxes, duties, imposts and excises, to pay the debts and provide for the common defence and general welfare of the United States;

but all duties, imposts and excises shall be uniform throughout the United States.

To borrow money on the credit of the United States;

To regulate commerce with foreign nations, and among the several states, and with the Indian tribes;

To establish a uniform rule of naturalization, and uniform laws on the subject of bankruptcies throughout the United States;

To coin money, regulate the value thereof, and of foreign coin, and fix the standard of weights and measures;

To provide for the punishment of counterfeiting the securities and current coin of the United States;

To establish post offices and post roads;

To promote the progress of science and useful arts, by securing for limited times to authors and inventors the exclusive right to their respective writings and discoveries.

To constitute tribunals inferior to the Supreme Court;

To define and punish piracies and felonies committed on the high seas, and offences against the law of nations;

To declare war, grant letters of marque and reprisal, and make rules concerning captures on land and water;

To raise and support armies, but *no appropriation* of money to that use *shall be for a longer term than two years;*

To provide and maintain a navy;

To make rules for the government and regulation of the land and naval forces;

To provide for calling forth the militia to execute the laws of the union, suppress insurrections and repel invasions;

To provide for organizing, arming, and disciplining, the militia, and for governing such part of them as may be employed in the service of the United States, reserving to the states respectively, the appointment of the officers, and the authority of training the militia according to the discipline prescribed by Congress;

To exercise exclusive legislation in all cases whatsoever, over such district (not exceeding ten miles square) as may, by cession of particular states, and the acceptance of Congress, become the seat of the government of the United States, and to exercise like authority over all places purchased by the consent of the legislature of the state in which the same shall be, for the erection of forts, magazines, arsenals, dock-yards, and other needful buildings;—And

To make all laws which shall be necessary and proper for carrying into execution the foregoing powers, and all other powers vested by this Constitution in the government of the United States, or in any department or officer thereof.

Section 9. The migration or importation of such persons as any of the states now existing shall think proper to admit, shall not be prohibited by the Congress prior to the year one thousand eight hundred and eight, but a tax or duty may be imposed on such importation, not exceeding ten dollars for each person.

The privilege of the writ of habeas corpus shall not be suspended, unless when in cases of rebellion or invasion the public safety may require it.

No bill of attainder or ex post facto law shall be passed.

No capitation, or other direct, tax shall be laid, unless in proportion to the census or enumeration herein before directed to be taken.

No tax or duty shall be laid on articles exported from any state.

No preference shall be given by any regulation of commerce or revenue to the ports of one state over those of another; nor shall vessels bound to, or from, one state, be obliged to enter, clear or pay duties in another.

No money shall be drawn from the Treasury, but in consequence of appropriations made by law; and a regular statement and account of the receipts and expenditures of all public money shall be published from time to time.

No title of nobility shall be granted by the United States: And no person holding any office of profit or trust under them, shall, without the consent of the Congress, accept of any present, emolument, office, or title, of any kind whatever, from any king, prince, or foreign state.

Section 10. *No state shall* enter into any treaty, alliance, or confederation; grant letters of marque and reprisal; coin money; emit bills of credit; make anything but gold and silver coin a tender in payment of debts; *pass any* bill of attainder, ex post facto law, or *law impairing the obligation of contracts,* or grant any title of nobility.

No state shall, without the consent of the Congress, lay any imposts or duties on imports or exports, except what may be absolutely necessary for executing its inspection laws: and the net produce of all duties and imposts, laid by any state on imports or exports, shall be for the use of the Treasury of the United States; and all such laws shall be subject to the revision and control of the Congress.

No state shall, without the consent of Congress, lay any duty of tonnage, keep troops, or ships of war in time of peace, enter into any agreement or compact with another state, or with a foreign power, or engage in war, unless actually invaded, or in such imminent danger as will not admit of delay.

ARTICLE II.

Section 1. The executive power shall be vested in a President of the United States of America. He shall hold his office during the term of four years, and, together with the Vice President, chosen for the same term, be elected, as follows:

Each state shall appoint, in such manner as the legislature thereof may direct, a number of electors, equal to the whole number of Senators and Representatives to which the state may be entitled in the Congress: but no Senator or Representative, or person holding an office of trust or profit under the United States, shall be appointed an elector.

~~The electors shall meet in their respective states, and vote by ballot for two persons, of whom one at least shall not be an inhabitant of the same state with themselves. And they shall make a list of all the persons voted for, and of the number of votes for each; which list they shall sign and certify, and transmit sealed to the seat of the government of the United States, directed to the President of the Senate. The President of the Senate shall, in the presence of the Senate and House of Representatives, open all the certificates, and the votes shall then be counted. The person having the~~

~~greatest number of votes shall be the President, if such number be a majority of the whole number of electors appointed, and if there be more than one who have such majority, and have an equal number of votes, then the House of Representatives shall immediately choose by ballot one of them for President; and if no person have a majority, then from the five highest on the list the said House shall in like manner choose the President. But in choosing the President, the votes shall be taken by states, the representation from each state having one vote; a quorum for this purpose shall consist of a member or members from two thirds of the states, and a majority of all the states shall be necessary to a choice. In every case, after the choice of the President, the person having the greatest number of votes of the electors shall be the Vice President. But if there should remain two or more who have equal votes, the Senate shall choose from them by ballot the Vice President.~~[5]

The Congress may determine the time of choosing the electors, and the day on which they shall give their votes; which day shall be the same throughout the United States.

No person except a natural born citizen, or a citizen of the United States, at the time of the adoption of this Constitution, shall be eligible to the office of President; neither shall any person be eligible to that office who shall not have attained to the age of thirty-five years, and been fourteen years a resident within the United States.

In case of the removal of the President from office, or of his death, resignation, or inability to discharge the powers and duties of the said office, the same shall devolve on the Vice President, and the Congress may by law provide for the case of removal, death, resignation or inability, both of the President and Vice President, declaring what officer shall then act as President, and such officer shall act accordingly, until the disability be removed, or a President shall be elected.

The President shall, at stated times, receive for his services, a compensation which shall neither be increased nor diminished during the period for which he shall have been elected, and he shall not

[5]Superseded by the 12th Amendment.

receive within that period any other emolument from the United States, or any of them.

Before he enter on the execution of his office, he shall take the following oath or affirmation:—"I do solemnly swear (or affirm) that I will faithfully execute the office of President of the United States, and will to the best of my ability, preserve, protect and defend the Constitution of the United States."

Section 2. The President shall be Commander in Chief of the Army and Navy of the United States, and of the militia of the several states, when called into the actual service of the United States; he may require the opinion, in writing, of the principal officer in each of the executive departments, upon any subject relating to the duties of their respective offices, and he shall have power to grant reprieves and pardons for offenses against the United States, except in cases of impeachment.

He shall have power, by and with the advice and consent of the Senate, to make treaties, provided two thirds of the Senators present concur; and he shall nominate, and *by and with the advice and consent of the Senate, shall appoint* ambassadors, other public ministers and consuls, Judges of the Supreme Court, and all other officers of the United States, whose appointments are not herein otherwise provided for, and which shall be established by law: but the Congress may by law vest the appointment of such inferior officers, as they think proper, in the President alone, in the courts of law, or in the heads of departments.

The President shall have power to fill up all vacancies that may happen during the recess of the Senate, by granting commissions which shall expire at the end of their next session.

Section 3. He shall from time to time give to the Congress information of the state of the union, and recommend to their consideration such measures as he shall judge necessary and expedient; he may, on extraordinary occasions, convene both Houses, or either of them, and in case of disagreement between them, with respect to the time of adjournment, he may adjourn them to such time as he shall think proper; he shall receive ambassadors and other public ministers; he shall take care that the laws be faithfully executed, and shall commission all the officers of the United States.

Section. 4 The President, Vice President and all civil officers of the United States, shall be removed from office on impeachment for, and conviction of, treason, bribery, or other high crimes and misdemeanors.

ARTICLE III.

Section 1. The judicial power of the United States, shall be vested in one Supreme Court, and in such inferior courts as the Congress may from time to time ordain and establish. *The Judges,* both of the supreme and inferior courts, *shall hold their offices during good behavior,* and shall, at stated times, receive for their services a compensation, which shall not be diminished during their continuance in office.

Section 2. The judicial power shall extend to all cases, in law and equity, arising under this Constitution, the laws of the United States, and treaties made, or which shall be made, under their authority;—to all cases affecting ambassadors, other public ministers and consuls;—to all cases of admiralty and maritime jurisdiction;—to controversies to which the United States shall be a party;—to controversies between two or more states;—~~between a state and citizens of another state;~~[6]—between citizens of different states;—between citizens of the same state claiming lands under grants of different states, ~~and between a state, or the citizens thereof, and foreign states, citizens or subjects.~~[7]

In all cases affecting ambassadors, other public ministers and consuls, and those in which a state shall be party, the Supreme Court shall have original jurisdiction. In all the other cases before mentioned, the Supreme Court shall have appellate jurisdiction, both as to law and fact, with such exceptions, and under such regulations as the Congress shall make.

The trial of all crimes, except in cases of impeachment, shall be by jury; and such trial shall be held in the state where the said crimes shall have been committed; but when not committed within any state, the trial shall be at such place or places as the Congress may by law have directed.

[6] See the 11th Amendment.

[7] *Ibid.*

Section 3. Treason against the United States shall consist only in levying war against them, or in adhering to their enemies, giving them aid and comfort. No person shall be convicted of treason unless on the testimony of two witnesses to the same overt act, or on confession in open court.

The Congress shall have power to declare the punishment of treason, but no attainder of treason shall work corruption of blood, or forfeiture except during the life of the person attainted.

ARTICLE IV.

Section 1. Full faith and credit shall be given in each state to the public acts, records, and judicial proceedings of every other state. And the Congress may by general laws prescribe the manner in which such acts, records and proceedings shall be proved, and the effect thereof.

Section 2. *The citizens of each state shall be entitled to all privileges and immunities of citizens in the several states.*

A person charged in any state with treason, felony, or other crime, who shall flee from justice, and be found in another state, shall on demand of the executive authority of the state from which he fled, be delivered up, to be removed to the state having jurisdiction of the crime.

~~No person held to service or labor in one state, under the laws thereof, escaping into another, shall, in consequence of any law or regulation therein, be discharged from such service or labor, but shall be delivered up on claim of the party to whom such service or labor may be due.~~[8]

Section 3. New states may be admitted by the Congress into this union; but no new state shall be formed or erected within the jurisdiction of any other state; nor any state be formed by the junction of two or more states, or parts of states, without the consent of the legislatures of the states concerned as well as of the Congress.

The Congress shall have power to dispose of and make all needful rules and regulations respecting the territory or other property belonging to the United States; and nothing in this Constitution

[8]See 13th Amendment.

shall be so construed as to prejudice any claims of the United States, or of any particular state.

Section 4. *The United States shall guarantee to every state in this union a republican form of government*, and *shall protect each of them against invasion;* and on application of the legislature, or of the executive (when the legislature cannot be convened) *against domestic violence.*

ARTICLE V.

The Congress, whenever two thirds of both Houses shall deem it necessary, *shall propose amendments* to this Constitution, or, on *the application* of the legislatures of *two thirds of the* several *states, shall call a convention for proposing amendments, which,* in either case, *shall be valid* to all intents and purposes, as part of this Constitution, *when ratified by* the legislatures of *three fourths of the several states,* or by conventions in three fourths thereof, as the one or the other mode of ratification may be proposed by the Congress; provided that no amendment which may be made prior to the year one thousand eight hundred and eight shall in any manner affect the first and fourth clauses in the ninth section of the first article; and that no state, without its consent, shall be deprived of its equal suffrage in the Senate.

ARTICLE VI.

All debts contracted and engagements entered into, betore the adoption of this Constitution, shall be as valid against the United States under this Constitution, as under the Confederation.

This Constitution, and the laws of the United States which shall be made in pursuance thereof; and all treaties made, or which shall be made, under the authority of the United States, *shall be the Supreme law of the land;* and the judges in every state shall be bound thereby, anything in the Constitution or laws of any state to the contrary notwithstanding.

The Senators and Representatives before mentioned, and the members of the several state legislatures, and all executive and judicial officers, both of the United States and of the several states, shall be bound by oath or affirmation, to support this Constitution; but no religious test shall ever be required as a qualification to any office or public trust under the United States.

ARTICLE VII.

The ratification of the conventions of nine states shall be sufficient for the establishment of this Constitution between the states so ratifying the same.

DONE in convention by the unanimous consent of the states present the seventeenth day of September in the year of our Lord one thousand seven hundred and eighty-seven and of the independence of the United States of America the twelfth in witness whereof we have hereunto subscribed our names.

G° Washington—Presidt.
and deputy from Virginia

New Hampshire	John Langdon Nicholas Gilman
Massachusetts	Nathaniel Gorham Rufus King
Connecticut	Wm. Saml. Johnson Roger Sherman
New York . . .	Alexander Hamilton
New Jersey	Wil: Livingston David Brearley. Wm. Paterson. Jona: Dayton

Pennsylvania	B Franklin Thomas Mifflin Robt Morris Geo. Clymer Thos. FitzSimons Jared Ingersoll James Wilson Gouv Morris
Delaware	Geo: Read Gunning Bedford jun John Dickinson Richard Bassett Jaco: Broom
Maryland	James McHenry Dan of St. Thos. Jenifer Danl Carroll
Virginia	John Blair— James Madison Jr.
North Carolina	Wm. Blount Richd. Dobbs Spaight. Hu Williamson
South Carolina	J. Rutledge Charles Cotesworth Pinckney Charles Pinckney Pierce Butler
Georgia	William Few Abr Baldwin

ARTICLES IN ADDITION TO, AND AMENDMENT OF, THE CONSTITUTION OF THE UNITED STATES OF AMERICA, PROPOSED BY CONGRESS, AND RATIFIED BY THE SEVERAL STATES, PURSUANT TO THE FIFTH ARTICLE OF THE ORIGINAL CONSTITUTION.

AMENDMENT I.

[Ratification of the first ten amendments was completed December 15, 1791.]

Congress shall make no law respecting an establishment of re-*ligion,* or prohibiting the free exercise thereof; or *abridging the freedom of speech, or of the press; or the right* of the people peaceably *to assemble, and to petition* the government for a redress of grievances.

AMENDMENT II.

A well regulated militia being necessary to the security of a free state, *the right* of the people *to keep and bear arms shall not be infringed.*

AMENDMENT III.

No soldier shall, in time of peace *be quartered in any house, without the consent of the owner,* nor in time of war, but in a manner to be prescribed by law.

AMENDMENT IV.

The right of the people to be secure in their persons, houses, papers, and effects, *against unreasonable searches and seizures, shall not be violated,* and no warrants shall issue, but upon probable cause, supported by oath or affirmation, and particularly describing the place to be searched, and the persons or things to be seized.

AMENDMENT V.

No person shall be held to answer for a capital, or otherwise infamous crime, unless on a presentment or *indictment of a grand jury,* except in cases arising in the land or naval forces, or in the militia, when in actual service in time of war or public danger;

nor shall any person be subject for the same offence to be twice put in jeopardy of life or limb; nor shall be compelled in any criminal case to be a witness against himself, nor be deprived of life, *liberty, or property, without due process of law; nor shall private property be taken for public use, without just compensation.*

AMENDMENT VI.

In all criminal prosecutions, the accused shall enjoy the right to a speedy and public trial, by an impartial jury of the state and district wherein the crime shall have been committed, which district shall have been previously ascertained by law, and to be informed of the nature and cause of the accusation; *to be confronted with the witness against him;* to have compulsory process for obtaining witness in his favor, and *to have the assistance of counsel* for his defence.

AMENDMENT VII.

In suits at common law, where the value in controversy shall exceed twenty dollars, the right of trial by jury shall be preserved, and no fact tried by a jury shall be otherwise re-examined in any court of the United States, than according to the rules of the common law.

AMENDMENT VIII.

Excessive bail shall not be required, nor excessive fines imposed, nor cruel and unusual punishments inflicted.

AMENDMENT IX.

The enumeration in the Constitution, of certain rights, shall not be construed to deny or disparage others retained by the people.

AMENDMENT X.

The powers not delegated to the United States by the Constitution, nor prohibited by it to the states, *are reserved to the states respectively, or to the people.*

AMENDMENT XI.

[January 8, 1798]

The judicial power of the United States shall not be construed to extend to any suit in law or equity, commenced or prosecuted against one of the United States by citizens of another state, or by citizens or subjects of any foreign state.

AMENDMENT XII.

[September 25, 1804]

The electors shall meet in their respective states and vote by ballot for President and Vice-President, one of whom, at least, shall not be an inhabitant of the same state with themselves! they shall name in their ballots the person voted for as President, and in distinct ballots the person voted for as Vice-President, and they shall make distinct lists of all persons voted for as President, and of all persons voted for as Vice-President, and of the number of votes for each, which lists they shall sign and certify, and transmit sealed to the seat of the government of the United States, directed to the President of the Senate;—the President of the Senate shall, in the presence of Senate and House of Representatives, open all the certificates and the votes shall then be counted;—the person having the greatest number of votes for President, shall be the President, if such number be a majority of the whole number of electors appointed; and if no person have such majority, then from the persons having the highest numbers not exceeding three on the list of those voted for as President, the House of Representatives shall choose immediately, by ballot, the President. But in choosing the President, the votes shall be taken by states, the representation from each state having one vote; a quorum for this purpose shall consist of a member or members from two-thirds of the states, and a majority of all the states shall be necessary to a choice. And if the House of Representatives shall not choose a President whenever the right of choice shall devolve upon them, ~~before the fourth day of March next following,~~[9] then the Vice-President shall act as President, as in the case of the death or other constitutional disability of the

[9]Altered by the 20th Amendment.

President. The person having the greatest number of votes as Vice-President, shall be the Vice-President, if such number be a majority of the whole number of electors appointed, and if no person have a majority, then from the two highest numbers on the list, the Senate shall choose the Vice-President; a quorum for the purpose shall consist of two-thirds of the whole number of Senators, and a majority of the whole number shall be necessary to a choice. But no person constitutionally ineligible to the office of President shall be eligible to that of Vice-President of the United States.

AMENDMENT XIII.

[December 18, 1865]

Section 1. *Neither slavery nor involuntary servitude,* except as a punishment for crime whereof the party shall have been duly convicted, *shall exist within the United States,* or any place subject to their jurisdiction.

Section 2. Congress shall have power to enforce this article by appropriate legislation.

AMENDMENT XIV.

[July 28, 1868]

Section 1. All persons born or naturalized in the United States, and subject to the jurisdiction thereof, are citizens of the United States and of the state wherein they reside. *No state shall* make or enforce any law which shall abridge the privileges or immunities of citizens of the United States; *nor shall any state deprive any person of life, liberty, or property, without due process of law;* nor *deny to any person within its jurisdiction the equal protection of the laws.*

Section 2. Representatives shall be apportioned among the several states according to their respective numbers, counting the whole number of persons in each state, excluding Indians not taxed. But when the right to vote at any election for the choice of electors for President and Vice President of the United States, Representatives in Congress, the executive and judicial officers of a state, or the members of the legislature thereof, is denied to any of the male inhabitants of such state, being twenty-one years of age, and citizens of the United States, or in any way abridged, except for participation in rebellion, or other crime, the basis of representation therein shall be reduced in the proportion which the number of such male citizens shall bear to the whole number of male citizens twenty-one years of age in such state.

Section 3. No person shall be a Senator or Representative in Congress, or elector of President and Vice President, or hold any office, civil or military, under the United States, or under any state, who, having previously taken an oath, as a member of Congress, or as an officer of the United States, or as a member of any state legislature, or as an executive or judicial officer of any state to support the Constitution of the United States, shall have engaged in insurrection or rebellion against the same, or given aid or comfort to the enemies thereof. But Congress may by a vote of two-thirds of each House, remove such disability.

Section 4. The validity of the public debt of the United States, authorized by law, including debts incurred for payment of pensions and bounties for services in suppressing insurrection or rebellion, shall not be questioned. But neither the United States nor any state shall assume or pay any debt or obligation incurred in aid of insurrection or rebellion against the United States, or any claim for the loss or emancipation of any slave; but all such debts, obligations and claims shall be held illegal and void.

Section 5. The Congress shall have power to enforce, by appropriate legislation, the provisions of this article.

AMENDMENT XV.
[March 30, 1870]

Section 1. The right of citizens of the United States to vote shall not be denied or abridged by the United States or by any state on account of race, color, or previous condition of servitude.

Section 2. The Congress shall have power to enforce this article by appropriate legislation.

AMENDMENT XVI.

[February 25, 1913]

The Congress shall have power to lay and collect taxes on incomes, from whatever source derived, without apportionment among the several states, and without regard to any census or enumeration.

AMENDMENT XVII.

[May 31, 1913]

The Senate of the United States shall be composed of two Senators from each state, elected by the people thereof, for six years; and each Senator shall have one vote. The electors in each state shall have the qualifications requisite for electors of the most numerous branch of the state legislatures.

When vacancies happen in the representation of any state in the Senate, the executive authority of such state shall issue writs of election to fill such vacancies: *Provided,* That the legislature of any state may empower the executive thereof to make temporary appointments until the people fill the vacancies by election as the legislature may direct.

This amendment shall not be so construed as to affect the election or term of any Senator chosen before it becomes valid as part of the Constitution.

AMENDMENT XVIII.

[January 29, 1919]

Section 1. ~~After one year from the ratification of this article the manufacture, sale, or transportation of intoxicating liquors within, the importation thereof into, or the exportation thereof from the United States and all territory subject to the jurisdiction thereof for beverage purposes is hereby prohibited.~~

Sec. 2. ~~The Congress and the several states shall have concurrent power to enforce this article by appropriate legislation.~~

Sec. 3. ~~This article shall be inoperative unless it shall have been ratified as an amendment to the Constitution by the legislatures of the several states, as provided in the Constitution, within seven years from the date of the submission hereof to the states by the Congress.~~[10]

[10] Repealed by the 21st amendment.

AMENDMENT XIX.

[August 26, 1920]

The right of citizens of the United States to vote shall not be denied or abridged by the United States or by any state on account of sex.

Congress shall have power to enforce this article by appropriate legislation.

AMENDMENT XX.

[February 6, 1933]

Section 1. The terms of the President and Vice President shall end at noon on the 20th day of January, and the terms of Senators and Representatives at noon on the 3d day of January, of the years in which such terms would have ended if this article had not been ratified; and the terms of their successors shall then begin.

Sec. 2. The Congress shall assemble at least once in every year, and such meeting shall begin at noon on the 3d day of January, unless they shall by law appoint a different day.

Sec. 3. If, at the time fixed for the beginning of the term of the President, the President elect shall have died, the Vice President elect shall become President. If a President shall not have been chosen before the time fixed for the beginning of his term, or if the President elect shall have failed to qualify, then the Vice President elect shall act as President until a President shall have qualified; and the Congress may by law provide for the case wherein neither a President elect nor a Vice President elect shall have qualified, declaring who shall then act as President, or the manner in which one who is to act shall be selected, and such person shall act accordingly until a President or Vice President shall have qualified.

Sec. 4. The Congress may by law provide for the case of the death of any of the persons from whom the House of Representatives may choose a President whenever the right of choice shall have devolved upon them, and for the case of the death of any of the persons from whom the Senate may choose a Vice President whenever the right of choice shall have devolved upon them.

Sec. 5. Sections 1 and 2 shall take effect on the 15th day of

October following the ratification of this article.

Sec. 6. This article shall be inoperative unless it shall have been ratified as an amendment to the Constitution by the legislatures of three-fourths of the several states within seven years from the date of its submission.

AMENDMENT XXI.

[December 5, 1933]

Section 1. The eighteenth article of amendment to the Constitution of the United States is hereby repealed.

Sec. 2. The transportation or importation into any state, territory, or possession of the United States for delivery or use therein of intoxicating liquors, in violation of the laws thereof, is hereby prohibited.

Sec. 3. This article shall be inoperative unless it shall have been ratified as an amendment to the Constitution by conventions in the several states, as provided in the Constitution, within seven years from the date of the submission hereof to the states by the Congress.

AMENDMENT XXII.

[February 27, 1951]

Section 1. No person shall be elected to the office of the President more than twice, and no person who has held the office of President, or acted as President, for more than two years of a term to which some other person was elected President shall be elected to the office of President more than once. But this article shall not apply to any person holding the office of President when this article was proposed by the Congress, and shall not prevent any person who may be holding the office of President, or acting as President, during the term within which this article becomes operative from holding the office of President or acting as President during the remainder of such term.

Sec. 2. This article shall be inoperative unless it shall have been ratified as an amendment to the Constitution by the legislatures of three-fourths of the several states within seven years from the date of its submission to the states by the Congress.

Index

*Index**

Amending process, 5, 10-11, 97, *117*
Arms, right to keep and bear, 44-45, *123*
Assembly, freedom of, 40, 42

Balances, 12-13
  and checks, 12-17, 97, *See also* Checks
Basic Principles of Your Government, Eight, 5, 9-29
Bills of attainder, protection against, 34-35, *114*

Checks:
  and balances, 12-17
  on Congress, 13-14, *109, 110, 111, 112*
  on the Federal Government, 16, *124*
  on the President, 14-15, *110, 111, 112, 113, 117*
  on the Supreme Court, 15, *110, 117, 118*
Communications, as factor of freedom, 90
Confidence, as factor of freedom, 90
Confrontation of accusers, right to, 50, 51, 52, *124*
Constitutional supremacy, 5, 18-19, 98, *120*
Constitution of the United States, text of, 109-130
Co-operation, as factor of freedom, 90
Counsel, right to services of, 51, 52, 53, *124*

***Page numbers in *italics* refer to passages in the Constitution.**

Courage, as factor of freedom, 90
Cruel and unusual punishment, protection against, 60-61, *124*
Culture, as factor of freedom, 90

Determination, as factor of freedom, 91
Discrimination, by one state against citizens of another, protection against, *76-77, 119*
Domestic uprising, protection from, 82-83, *120*
Double jeopardy, protection against, *56-57, 124*
Dual form of government, 5, 19-20, 99, *112-14, 120, 124*
Due process of law, 66-67, *124, 126*

Education, as factor of freedom, 91
Eight Basic Principles of Your Government, 5, *9-29*
Entrance into and exit from states, 80-81
Equality before the law, 36-37, *119, 126*
Equal protection of laws, 70-71, *126*
Exalted judiciary, 5, 22-23, 100
Excessive bail, protection against, 60-61, *124*
Ex post facto laws, protection against, 38-39, *114*

Faith, as factor of freedom, 91
Family, as factor of freedom, 91
Foreign invasion, protection from, 82-83, *120*

Freedom:
Instruments of, vs. Instruments of Tyranny, 31-85
of assembly, 40, 42
of petition, 43
of press, 40, 42, *123*
of religion, 40-41
of speech, 40, 41
Freedoms, civil and political, 5, 24-25, 101

Generosity, as factor of freedom, 91
Genius of American People, as factor of freedom, 91-92
Government of limited powers, 5, 26-27, 101-102
Grand jury indictment, 50-51, *123*
Guarantees, Twenty-Five, 31-85

Habeas corpus, writ of, 32-33, *114*
Health, as factor of freedom, 92
Hope, as factor of freedom, 92
How to Play Your Part, 87-105
How you "let freedom ring," 96-105

Initiative, as factor of freedom, 92-93
Instruments of Freedom vs. Instruments of Tyranny, 31-85
Instruments of a Republic, 87-105
"Instruments of your republic," 6-8
Involuntary servitude, protection against, 74-75, *126*

Labor, as factor of freedom, 93
Leadership, as factor of freedom, 93
Life, liberty and property, right to, 50-53, *124*

"Live wires," 88-95
Loyalty, as factor of freedom, 94

Management, as factor of freedom, 94
Mutual respect, as factor of freedom, 94

Petition, freedom of, 43
Press, freedom of, 40, 42, *123*
Property taken for public use,
compensation, 62-63, *124*

Quartering of troops, protection
against, 46-47, *123*

Religion, freedom of, 40-41
Religious tests for holding public office,
protection against, 78-79, *121*
Republican form of government, 5,
28-29, 102-104, *120*, *127*, *129*
in your state, 72-73, *120*
Resources, as factor of freedom, 94
Responsibility, as factor of freedom, 94
Rewards, as factor of freedom, 94
Right to vote, protection of, 84-85, *127*,
129

Sanctity of contracts, 68-69, *115*
Savings, as factor of freedom, 95
Self-incrimination, protection against,
58-59, *124*
Skillfulness, as factor of freedom, 95
Slavery, protection against, 74-75, *126*
Speech, freedom of, 40-41
Spirituality, as factor of freedom, 95
Subpoena, power of, 51, 52, 53, *124*
"Sweet Freedom's Song," 2-8

Titles of nobility, 36-37, *114*

Tools of production, as factor of freedom, 95
Trial, right to a speedy and public, 54-55, *124*
Trial by jury, right to in civil cases, 61-65, *124*
Twenty-Five Guarantees, 31-85

Unreasonable search and seizure, protection against, 48, *123*
United States Constitution, text of, 109-130

Voting, privilege of, 84-85

Writ of habeas corpus, 32-33, *114*